What's So Great About . . . ?

ANNE FRANK

Jim Whiting

Mitchell Lane
PUBLISHERS

P.O. Box 196
Hockessin, Delaware 19707
Visit us on the web: www.mitchelllane.com
Comments? email us: mitchelllane@mitchelllane.com

Mitchell Lane PUBLISHERS

Printing   1   2   3   4   5   6   7   8   9

A Robbie Reader/What's So Great About . . . ?

Amelia Earhart	**Anne Frank**	Annie Oakley
Christopher Columbus	Daniel Boone	Davy Crockett
Elizabeth Blackwell	Ferdinand Magellan	Francis Scott Key
Galileo	George Washington Carver	Harriet Tubman
Helen Keller	Henry Hudson	Jacques Cartier
Johnny Appleseed	Paul Bunyan	Robert Fulton
Rosa Parks	Sam Houston	

Library of Congress Cataloging-in-Publication Data
Whiting, Jim.
   Anne Frank / by Jim Whiting.
     p. cm. — (A Robbie reader. What's so great about . . . ?)
   Includes bibliographical references and index.
   ISBN 978-1-58415-581-2 (library bound)
   1. Frank, Anne, 1929–1945—Juvenile literature. 2. Jewish children in the Holocaust—Netherlands—Amsterdam—Biography—Juvenile literature. 3. Jews—Netherlands—Amsterdam—Biography—Juvenile literature. 4. Holocaust, Jewish (1939–1945)—Netherlands—Amsterdam—Biography—Juvenile literature. I. Title.
DS135.N6F73865 2007
940.53'18092—dc22
[B]
                                           2007000818

ABOUT THE AUTHOR: Jim Whiting has been a remarkably versatile and accomplished journalist, writer, editor, and photographer for more than 30 years. He has written and edited more than 250 nonfiction children's books. His subjects range from authors to zoologists and include contemporary pop icons and classical musicians, saints and scientists, emperors and explorers. Representative titles include *The Life and Times of Franz Liszt, The Life and Times of Julius Caesar, Charles Schulz, Charles Darwin and the Origin of the Species, Juan Ponce de Leon, Robert Fulton,* and *The Scopes Monkey Trial.* He lives in Washington State with his wife and two teenage sons.

PPC

TABLE OF CONTENTS

Words in **bold** type can be found in the glossary.

Anne Frank stands between her parents, Otto Frank and Edith Frank. Margot stands at the left in the picture, which was taken in Amsterdam, the Netherlands, in 1941.

A Nighttime Scare

Anne Frank was frightened. It was almost midnight, and it sounded like someone was trying to break in.

"Footsteps in the house," she wrote. "The private office, the kitchen, then . . . on the staircase."

Anne wasn't by herself. Her parents and her sister were with her. So were Hermann and Auguste van Pels, their son Peter, and Fritz Pfeffer, a family friend.

"All sounds of breathing stopped, eight hearts pounded," she continued. "Footsteps on the stairs . . . then we heard a can fall, and the footsteps **receded**."

They didn't know if they were still in danger. "A shiver went through everyone's body. I heard several sets of teeth chattering, no one said a word," Anne continued.

A home break-in would be frightening for anyone. For Anne and the others, it would almost certainly mean death. This incident took place during World War II in April 1944 in Amsterdam, Holland. At that time, Holland was controlled by Germany, whose leader was Adolf Hitler.

Hitler disliked Jews—people who practice **Judaism** (JOO-day-ism). When he came to power in 1933, he ordered restrictions to be placed on them. Many Jews were arrested and taken to **concentration camps**. In these awful places, thousands of people were crammed together in filthy conditions. Many starved to death or died from disease. Most of the others were killed. This evil program became known as the **Holocaust** (HAH-luh-kost).

The Franks and the others were Jewish. They had been hiding from the Germans for

In German concentration camps, men and women were separated. Their hair was shaved, and their clothes, jewels, and money were taken. They were given thin clothing and a bowl, then sent to live in overcrowded bunkhouses. Many died of starvation or disease.

nearly two years. They knew that if they were discovered, they too would be sent to concentration camps.

They had taken a radio with them into hiding and listened to it every day. In the months before the break-in, the news had gotten better. They heard that the Germans were losing the war. When the Germans were finally defeated, they would be safe. Could they stay hidden that long?

Anne Frank sits on her sister Margot's lap. The picture was taken while the family was still living in Frankfurt, Germany. Anne is about three years old.

Growing Up Under a Shadow

Anne Frank was born on June 12, 1929, in Frankfurt, Germany. Her parents were Otto and Edith Frank. Anne joined a sister, Margot, who was three years older.

World War I had ended more than ten years earlier, and Germans were still bitter about losing it. Adolf Hitler took advantage of that bitterness by promising to make Germans feel proud again. One of his tactics was to blame Jews for many of the country's problems. His stories were lies, but many people believed him.

Otto Frank, like many others, was afraid of Hitler and his police force. In 1933, he moved his family to Amsterdam, which was known for its religious freedom.

For several years, it looked as if Otto had made the right decision. His business was successful. Anne and Margot learned to speak Dutch and made many friends. Later, Anne described those days as "heavenly." She had "five admirers on every street corner, twenty or so friends, the favorite of most of my teachers, spoiled rotten by Father and Mother, bags full of candy and a big allowance. What more could anyone ask for?"

She soon found out. When the German army conquered Holland in May 1940, restrictions were placed on Jews who lived there. They had to wear yellow **Stars of David**. Anne and Margot were forced to drop out of their school and attend one limited to Jews. Their father had to give up his business.

Otto Frank tried to make life as normal as he could. Celebrating birthdays was part of a normal life. When Anne turned thirteen on June 12, 1942, he made sure the day was

After the Germans took over Holland in 1940, they forced Jews to wear badges. The word *Jood* means "Jew" in Dutch.

special. Anne received many presents: flowers, a blue blouse, a puzzle, three books, cookies and candy–and a diary.

That very day, she made her first diary entry. "I hope I will be able to **confide** everything to you, as I have never been able to confide in anyone, and I hope you will be a great source of comfort and support," she wrote.

Anne Frank had no way of knowing that she had begun one of the most famous books in history.

The Anne Frank House in Amsterdam. The Franks hid in The Annex, which is located in the rear of the building. In 1960, the Anne Frank House was opened to the public as a museum.

Into the Annex

For months, Otto had been trying to get his family to safety. He wrote dozens of desperate letters, pleading for help in getting his family out of the country. Nothing worked. Because it was impossible to leave Holland, he figured out another plan.

A few weeks after Anne's birthday, Margot received an official letter. It ordered her to go to a work camp. Jews had heard frightening stories about these work camps. Many people went in, but hardly anyone came out. Otto had no intention of letting Margot report for "duty."

It was time to put his plan in action. On July 6, 1942, the family woke up early. Even though it was a hot day, they put on as many clothes as they could and walked out the front door. Their destination was the building that housed Otto's old business. The building had a rear extension called The Annex. It was screened from view by houses on all sides. Hardly anyone even knew it was there. Otto thought it would be a good hiding place.

Otto's former employees liked him a lot. They secretly helped him set up The Annex. No one else could know their plans—and that is why the Franks wore so much clothing that morning. It was the only way to take it with them. They couldn't carry suitcases, or the patrolling soldiers would have known they were going somewhere.

Once they were inside, a bookcase concealed the door. They had to be very quiet during the day, when people were downstairs doing business. They couldn't flush the toilet or run water until the evening, when everyone downstairs had gone home.

The employees continued to help them. They kept them supplied with food and other

A reconstruction of the bookcase that concealed the entrance to The Annex. The bookcase could be moved to enable the hideaways' friends to bring them food and other supplies.

essentials (ee-SEN-chuls). Shortly after the Franks went into hiding, the employees also brought the Van Pels family and Pfeffer. It was extremely dangerous for everyone involved. Helping Jews was a serious crime.

The Franks and their friends settled down to wait. They couldn't go outside. They knew the only thing that could save them was the Germans' losing the war. They knew it would be a long wait.

Anne Frank writes at her desk in 1940. The German
soldiers had just arrived in Holland. Within two years,
Anne would go into hiding.

Living in Constant Fear

The days and weeks and months went by. It was hard for eight people to be cooped up for so long. They often argued. Anne did everything she could to stay happy.

She loved to talk. Often the others didn't want to listen to her. Sometimes they **criticized** her. She knew that she could trust her diary. She wrote about the details of her daily life.

"I washed mother's hair this evening, which is no easy task these days because there's no more shampoo," read one entry. "This morning I made two cakes and a batch of cookies," read another.

Sometimes they had fun. One day Peter wore his mother's dress and Anne put on

Peter van Pels was one of the eight people hiding in The Annex. He was about two and a half years older than Anne. At first she wasn't very impressed with him. Eventually she fell in love with him, and he was the first boy to kiss her.

Peter's suit. "The grown-ups split their sides laughing, and we enjoyed ourselves every bit as much," she wrote.

Soon she filled up the diary her father had given her. She didn't want to stop writing, so she used notebooks and loose pieces of paper.

One night in March 1944, she heard a radio broadcast from important Dutch officials. The officials had escaped and gone to England. They wanted letters and diaries from people still living in Holland. They would print them when the war was over. It would show the world how much the Dutch people had suffered.

From that moment, Anne knew she wanted to publish her diary. She became very excited and began making some changes. For example, Pfeffer's name was changed to Albert Düssell. She changed the name of the Van Pels family to Van Daan.

She became especially excited on June 6, 1944. The radio reported that American, British, and Canadian soldiers had landed in

When the Franks and their friends were found, they knew they would be shipped from Amsterdam to one of the camps run by Hitler's army.

American soldiers wade ashore in France on D-day, the morning of June 6, 1944. Despite heavy losses, the Americans and their British and Canadian allies established a beachhead. It would take until spring 1945 for them to free the concentration camps.

France. "I have the feeling that friends are on the way," she wrote. "Maybe, Margot says, I can even go back to school in October or September."

Anne Frank would never go back to school. On August 4, 1944, German policemen pounded on the door. Someone had **betrayed** the eight people hiding in The Annex.

A scene from the film *The Diary of Anne Frank*, featuring Joseph Schildkraut (standing left, as Otto Frank), Ed Wynn (standing right, as Albert Düssell), Millie Perkins (as Anne Frank), and Richard Beymer (on the floor, as Peter van Daan).

Anne's Words Live On

No one knows who gave them up. The Germans allowed the hideaways a few moments to gather some belongings. Then they took the eight prisoners outside to a van, which drove them to a prison camp in Holland.

As they normally did, the Germans seized everything they thought was valuable in The Annex. Anne's notebooks and papers did not appear to be worth anything. The Germans didn't bother picking them up. A few men even trampled on them. Miep Gies, one of the people who had risked her life to help the Franks, found them later and saved them.

A few weeks after the arrest, a train carried Anne, her family, and her friends to

In a scene from the film *The Diary of Anne Frank*, a soldier searches for the entrance to The Annex. Only fourteen years after the war, Anne's moving, terrifying story had been made into a film.

Otto Frank sits with Miep Gies (left) sometime in 1941. Miep was a close family friend who helped the Franks while they were hiding, even though she knew it was risky for her. She received several awards for her bravery.

Auschwitz (OUSH-vitz), one of the harshest German concentration camps. Two months later, Anne and Margot were transferred to the Bergen-Belsen concentration camp. Food and water were rarely provided. It was very cold in the winter. The prisoners lived in dirt and filth, and many people got sick. In February or

March in 1945, Margot died. Anne died a few days later.

Somehow their father survived. He was the only one of the eight who did. Their mother, Pfeffer, and all three members of the Van Pels family perished in the concentration camps.

When Otto was freed after the German surrender, he returned to The Annex. Miep Gies gave him Anne's diary. He opened it and began reading. Soon he was crying.

A statue of Anne Frank stands close to the Anne Frank House.

He decided to share her diary with the world. It was published in 1947. Since then, it has been translated into many languages, and movies and plays have been produced. Millions of people have read Anne's story.

Anne put a human face on the Holocaust. Her diary

Both Anne and her sister, Margot, died in the Bergen-Belsen concentration camp. Most victims were thrown into mass graves, so no one knows where Anne and Margot were buried. This memorial is located near several of the mass graves.

showed that the victims weren't just numbers. They were real people who lived and loved and laughed.

In one of her earliest entries, Anne wrote, "It seems to me that later on neither I nor anyone else will be interested in the **musings** of a thirteen-year-old schoolgirl."

Anne was wrong. *The Diary of Anne Frank* became one of the most important books of the twentieth century.

CHRONOLOGY

1929   Anne Frank is born on June 12 in Frankfurt, Germany.

1933   Anne and her family move to Amsterdam, Holland.

1942

June 12	Anne begins her diary.
July 6	Anne and her family go into hiding in The Annex.

1944

March 29	Anne decides to publish her diary.
August 1	Anne makes the last entry in her diary.
August 4	Anne, her family, and her friends are arrested.

1945   Margot and Anne die in late February or early March. The Germans surrender, and Otto Frank is freed.

1947   Anne's diary is published in Dutch as *The Annex*.

1952   The diary is published in the United States as *Diary of a Young Girl*.

1955   The play *The Diary of Anne Frank* opens in New York City and wins several awards.

1959   The movie version of *A Diary of Anne Frank* is released and wins three Academy Awards.

1960   The Anne Frank House in Amsterdam becomes a museum.

1980   Otto Frank dies.

2007   Anne Frank's cousin Bernhard Elias donates thousands of letters, photographs, and documents to the Anne Frank House. They include Otto Frank's 1945 letter telling his mother in Switzerland that Anne, Margot, and his wife, Edith, died in Nazi concentration camps. They also include photographs from the late 1890s of the Frank family in Frankfurt, Germany.

TIMELINE IN HISTORY

1889	Adolf Hitler is born in Austria.
1914	World War I begins.
1918	World War I ends.
1933	Adolf Hitler comes to power and establishes the first concentration camps.
1935	The Nuremberg Laws begin official discrimination against Jews.
1937	Restrictive laws close nearly every profession in Germany to Jews.
1939	Hitler begins World War II by invading Poland.
1940	Auschwitz, the largest German concentration camp, is opened in Poland.
1941	At Hitler's orders, the German army invades the Soviet Union.
1945	

	January	The Soviet army frees the first concentration camp, Auschwitz-Birkenau.
	April	Hitler commits suicide.
	May	World War II ends in Europe.
	October	Main Nazi leaders are placed on trial in Nuremberg, Germany.

1946	The Nuremberg Trials end with most Nazi leaders found guilty of war crimes.
1948	The Jewish nation of Israel is created.
1993	*Schindler's List*, a movie about a man who saved more than 1,000 Jews from concentration camps, wins Best Picture at the Academy Awards.
2005	World leaders gather at Auschwitz to commemorate the sixtieth anniversary of its liberation.
2007	The European Union passes laws making it a crime to deny the existence of the Holocaust.

FIND OUT MORE

Books

Frank, Anne. *The Diary of a Young Girl*. Translated by Susan Massotty. Edited by Otto H. Frank and Mirjam Pressler. New York: Bantam Books, 1997.

Hurwitz, Johanna. *Anne Frank: Life in Hiding*. New York: HarperTrophy, 1999.

Lewis, Brenda Ralph. *The Story of Anne Frank*. New York: Dorling Kindersley, 2001.

Poole, Josephine. *Anne Frank*. New York: Knopf Books for Young Readers, 2005.

Verhoeven, Rian, and Ruud Van der Rol. *Anne Frank: Beyond the Diary—A Photographic Remembrance*. Translated by Tony Langham. New York: Puffin Books, 1995.

Works Consulted

Anne Frank Center http://www.annefrank.com/

Anne Frank Museum Amsterdam http://www.annefrank.org/content.asp?pid=1&lid=2

Anne Frank the Writer—An Unfinished Story http://www.ushmm.org/museum/exhibit/online/af/htmlsite/

Denenberg, Barry. *Shadow Life: A Portrait of Anne Frank and Her Family*. New York: Scholastic Press, 2005.

Frank, Anne. *The Diary of a Young Girl*. Translated by Susan Massotty. Edited by Otto H. Frank and Mirjam Pressler. New York: Bantam Books, 1997.

Lindwer, Willy. *The Last Seven Months of Anne Frank*. Translated by Alison Meersschaert. New York: Anchor Books, 1991.

Max, Arthur. "Anne Frank's Cousin Donates Family Files." Associated Press, June 25, 2007. http://www.nysun.com/article/57336

Yahoo News. "Letters from Anne Frank's Father Surface," January 25, 2007. http://hnn.us/roundup/archives/41/2007/1/#34582

On the Internet
Anne Frank Center
   http://www.annefrank.com/
Anne Frank House
   http://www.annefrank.org/
The MyHero Project—Anne Frank
   http://myhero.com/myhero/hero.asp?hero=anne_frank
Stories of Survival—Children of the Holocaust
   http://www.adl.org/children_holocaust/children_main.asp

GLOSSARY

betrayed (bee-TRAYD)—Given to an enemy.

concentration (kon-sen-TRAY-shun) **camps**—Areas where large numbers of people are confined with little regard for their health or safety.

confide (kun-FYD)—Share a secret with.

criticized (KRIH-tih-syzd)—Found fault with.

essentials (ee-SEN-chuls)—Things that are necessary.

Holocaust (HAH-luh-kost)— Hitler's program to kill as many Jews as possible. It is estimated that up to six million Jews died during that time.

Judaism (JOO-day-ism)—A religion based on ancient Hebrew writings that teach there is only one God.

musings (MYOO-zings)—Thoughts.

receded (ree-SEE-did)—Slowly went away.

Stars of David—Six-sided stars that are a symbol of the Jewish faith.

INDEX